THE STORY OF A BUTTERFLY

Words by Margaret Rose Reed   Pictures by Manu Montoya

sourcebooks
eXplore

Published by Sourcebooks eXplore an imprint of Sourcebooks Kids
P.O. Box 4410, Naperville, Illinois 60567-4410
(630) 961-3900
sourcebookskids.com

Cataloging-in-Publication Data is on file with the Library of Congress.

Source of Production: 1010 Printing Asia Limited, Kwun Tong, Hong Kong, China
Date of Production: May 2023
Run Number: 5032492

Printed and bound in China.
OGP 10 9 8 7 6 5 4 3 2

Painted ladies are the perfect butterflies to study in schools to demonstrate metamorphosis.

"I've never seen a real painted lady before, but I've been reading books about them since I was little.

Here are some of its eggs!"

Butterflies start as tiny eggs laid on special leaves.

"I found a caterpillar!"

Once the egg hatches, out comes a caterpillar, or larva, that immediately begins eating the leaf it was born on.

"Look at all the different caterpillars!
They are so pretty."

Caterpillars come in many different sizes and
colors for the kind of butterfly they will become.

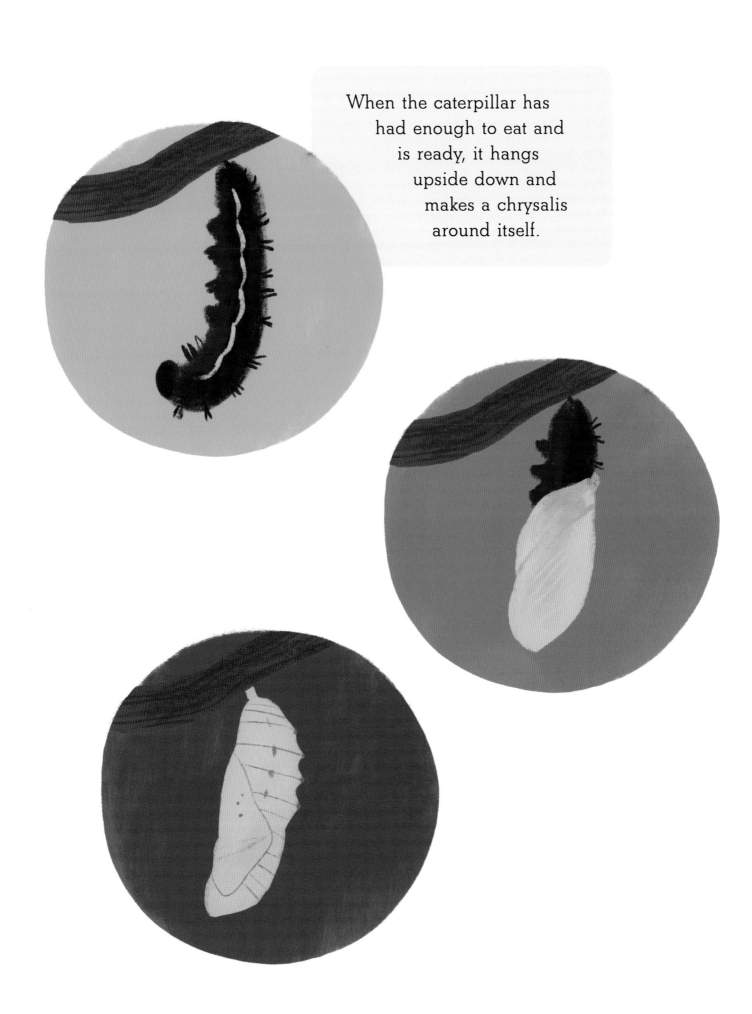

When the caterpillar has had enough to eat and is ready, it hangs upside down and makes a chrysalis around itself.

A caterpillar remains in a chrysalis for about a week. Inside, the caterpillar turns into goo, and the goo transforms into a butterfly!

"What could possibly be going on in there to change a caterpillar into a butterfly?"

"Something a little bit like magic happens!"

Once the metamorphosis is complete, the new butterfly needs to break out of the chrysalis. It cannot fly away yet though! First it must stretch its wings and dry out.

Butterflies eat with a proboscis, which is a straw-like tongue! Instead of having a nose to smell, butterflies detect scents through many different parts of their bodies including their legs!

Just like we couldn't start eating leaves and grass without getting sick, butterflies need to eat certain types of foods to stay strong and healthy. They are also particular about where they lay their eggs, so that as soon as the larvae emerge, they can begin to eat right away. We need to have the right types of "native" plants in order to have caterpillars and butterflies.

Native plants are plants that occur naturally in the area where they are growing.

"What if..."

Butterflies wanted! Please help us make a garden for butterflies and their caterpillars

Everyone in the community can join together to help make a place where butterflies and people thrive!

COMMUNITY BUTTERFLY GARDEN

Learn more about the PAINTED LADY BUTTERFLY!

VANESSA CARDUI

The painted lady's scientific name is *Vanessa cardui*. It's a butterfly found throughout most of the world except Antarctica and Australia. It is a beautiful orange-brown butterfly that scientists have studied closely because of its amazing characteristics and behaviors.

LIFE CYCLE

Egg

Adult Butterfly

Larva/Caterpillar

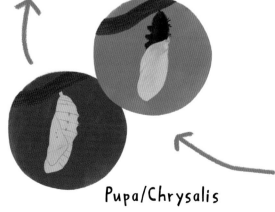

Pupa/Chrysalis

🦋 The painted lady's life cycle consists of four stages and is less than a month in total.

🦋 About three or four days after a female painted lady butterfly lays an egg, the larva, or caterpillar, eats its way out of the egg.

🦋 For the next few days, it continues to eat and eat some more. When it has eaten enough and is big and strong, it is ready to pupate. That means to make a chrysalis. The caterpillar will hang in a "J" shape and begin to make the chrysalis where it will become a butterfly.

🦋 The chrysalis will hang for about seven to fourteen days with no movement. Within the chrysalis, the caterpillar is changing into a butterfly in a process called metamorphosis. There are special cells in the caterpillar that remain there when it turns into a liquid in the chrysalis. Those special cells grow into a butterfly.

🦋 When it is ready, the butterfly pushes the chrysalis from the inside and it splits open. Slowly the butterfly emerges, but it has soft, wet, crumpled up wings that need to unfold and dry.

🦋 The painted lady life span is about two weeks after it comes out of the chrysalis. During that time, it finds a mate, lays eggs, and the cycle continues.

CHARACTERISTICS

The adult painted lady is about five to seven centimeters in length. The top part of the wing is orange-brown with a white bar on the front and a row of five tiny black dots on the back. The bottom parts of the wings have brown, black, and grey patterns with tiny spots. The eggs are a light green color and are as small as the tip of a pin. The caterpillar is greyish brown and dark at the end with a yellow stripe and spikes along the back and sides of its body.

The painted lady can adjust to living in many different types of habitats but loves to live in wide open areas such as fields and meadows of local plants and flowers.

There is a variety of hostplants that the painted lady likes, including thistle, hallows, hollyhock, and asters. Many butterflies are particular about their host plants, but the painted lady has a diverse range of plants that it can eat, which is good for its survival.

BEHAVIOR

Every year, painted lady butterflies make migrations from Africa to Europe and back again, and in North America from Mexico to the northern United States and Canada and back. Their migrations can be 7,500–9,000 miles long! This is the longest distance that any butterfly migrates. It helps being able to fly up to thirty miles per hour!

This migration does not happen in the lifetime of one butterfly. The butterflies make this round-trip journey over the course of about six generations! Think about it...one butterfly on a journey makes a stop to lay an egg. As that butterfly's life ends, the new life of the butterfly that formed from the caterpillar continues the same journey from where the mother butterfly left off. And this happens six times! How do those baby butterflies know what to do or where to go? Every generation must fly across a landscape that is has never seen! This migration is another wonder of nature.

What is the difference between butterflies and moths?

Behavior

BUTTERFLY	MOTH
Diurnal – most butterflies fly during the day	Nocturnal – most moths fly during the night

Fun Fact

Queen Alexandra's birdwing is the largest species of butterfly in the world, with a wingspan of eleven inches. It is an endangered species that only lives on Papua New Guinea.

BUTTERFLY

Anatomy

BUTTERFLY	MOTH
Does not have a frenulum	Has a frenulum, which joins the wings so they work together while flying

Antennae

BUTTERFLY	MOTH
Club shaped with a long shaft and a bulb at the end	Feathery and saw-edged

Wings

BUTTERFLY	MOTH
Folds wings vertically up over back	Holds wings in tent-like fashion that hides the body

MOTH

Chrysalis vs. Cocoon

BUTTERFLY	MOTH
Makes a chrysalis that is hard and smooth	Makes a cocoon that is wrapped in a silk covering

Fun Fact

There are many more species of moths than butterflies.

Fun Fact

It is not true that if you touch a butterfly's wing, the "powder" comes off and the butterfly will not be able to fly. It can still fly!

Fun Fact

The largest known moths are the Atlas moths, which have the greatest wing area, and the "white witch" moths with wingspans of twelves inches!